START BEING HAPPY

PROVEN PRACTICES FOR A JOYFUL LIFE

JUSTINE ROACH

Copyright © Justine Roach (2018)

2nd Edition 2020

The right of Justine Roach to be identified as the author of this work has been asserted by her.

Cover design by Austin Macauley Publishers Ltd

Published by Loyalty Publishing

Paperback ISBN: 978-0-6489056-0-8

Ebook Epub ISBN: 978-0-6489056-1-5

Ebook Mobi ISBN: 978-0-6489056-2-2

 A catalogue record for this book is available from the National Library of Australia

All rights reserved. No part of this book may be reproduced, stored in a retrieval system, or transmitted in any form or by any means: electronic, mechanical, photocopying, recording or otherwise, without the prior consent of the publisher.

The information in this book should not be treated as a substitute for professional medical advice; always consult a medical practitioner. Any use of information in this book is at the reader's discretion and risk. The author cannot be held responsible for any loss, claim or damage arising out of the use, or misuse, of the suggestions made, the failure to take medical advice or for any material on third party websites.

CONTENTS

About the Author — v

1. Introduction — 1
2. Set The Intention — 9
3. Find Twenty Minutes For Yourself Daily — 15
4. The World Is Our Mirror — 23
5. The Importance Of Reframing — 31
6. Don't Do Anything That Doesn't Lift Your Energy — 35
7. Pay Attention To Every Thought And Word — 45
8. Find Your Passion — 51
9. Evaluate Belief Systems — 57
10. Don't Shoot The Messenger — 69
11. We Are Four Body Beings — 81
12. Be Willing To Forgive — 89
13. Listen To The Masters — 97
14. Conclusion — 105

Acknowledgments — 111
Bibliography — 113

ABOUT THE AUTHOR

Justine runs a successful marketing agency with her husband Simon. She is a serial home renovator, proud mother and now author.

Her passion for emotional and spiritual growth inspired Justine's journey from struggle to empowerment. Encouraging and enlightening, Justine's writing comes from her heart and reflects her life changing philosophy.

This book is dedicated with deepest gratitude to my teacher, Barbara Andrews, who taught me everything written here with the tenderness and patience of the Divine Mother.

Happiness can come in a single moment. And in a single moment it can go again. But a single moment does not create it. Happiness is created through countless choices made and then made again throughout a lifetime.

— STEPHANIE DOWRICK

1
INTRODUCTION

We all want to be well rounded, happy individuals with the ability to cope with everything life presents us with. Yet, as children, many of us were not often given the emotional skill set required for this.

In the Western world, we tend to focus on academic competence as the foundation for our adult lives – but what about the tools we need to navigate the many and varied emotional landscapes we experience?

From early childhood until our deathbed, we experience uncomfortable or painful thoughts and feelings and we tend to either run from them, or try and 'sort them out in our head'.

For some of us, this mental approach may work. But there often comes a time, from my experience it tends to be around our late thirties and forties, when we start to want more joy and fulfilment in our lives and we begin our search for it.

Or, we may be presented with a life challenge that is so big, so frightening, so heartbreaking that it forces us to start looking at life in another way.

A crisis or an awakening gives us the opportunity to grow, to expand our view of the world and ourselves. It pushes us to realise that we are more than just three dimensional beings, where the physical realm is the only reality we are aware of. We begin to understand that we are multi- dimensional beings with extraordinary spirits, and often unexplored potential. A crisis has the capacity to shift us, albeit painfully, from the tribal, unconscious mind and into our full power as we learn to take personal responsibility for every one of our actions and reactions.

When we allow ourselves to consider this concept, it starts opening doors to a whole new world, a world that is infinitely richer, more expansive and creative than the one we have previously occupied.

In recognising that we are more than our physical bodies, we become aware of the presence of our soul and the enormous potential within us to create the life of our choice.

We start to recognise our own power and in doing so, we realise we have control over how we experience our lives. We stop being victims of circumstance and we start to take personal responsibility for the situations we find ourselves in. We begin to trust in our ability to effect the change we desire.

But, how do we start to access our full potential? Where is the blueprint that shows us the way?

This book is your road map. It is a practical guide that contains pragmatic techniques that, if practiced, will open the doorway to greater personal joy.

I know the practices in this book work because they changed my life over the course of ten years.

I started searching for a more fulfilling and contented life as a woman in my late thirties. I was functioning as a mother, wife and friend but I wasn't happy. Even though I was healthy, I was loved and I was financially secure, I was also miserable. Like many of us, I couldn't shake myself out of it.

In my mid-thirties, I had lost my best friend and sister, Rachael, to suicide. Her death was a terrible shock to me and without her beside me, the world became a very frightening and lonely place. I was 14 months older than Rachael but she had been my security blanket since I was a child. We were intrinsically connected, I had always relied on her for my emotional well-being and I had just assumed we would grow old together.

Several months after she died, I had a breakdown and three years later I was still struggling to recover. Rachael and I had been so entwined for 35 years and I didn't know how to live happily without her.

My sister's suicide didn't just have a terrible impact on me; it had a knock on effect on my son and husband because I changed so much after it. My son was very anxious and my husband felt very isolated. One day out of the blue, on the way home from visiting friends, my husband told me he wasn't happy in our marriage any more.

I felt like the rug had been pulled out from under me. We had been together for 17 years and whilst I wasn't feeling close to him at the time, I felt sick at the thought of him leaving me. I asked him what he wasn't happy with.

"Well," he said, "you used to be happy and sexy and we had fun together. Now you're miserable, you live in sports gear most of the time and we hardly ever have fun. I didn't sign up for this."

Even though I didn't like what my husband said, I knew it was true. I had lost touch with who I was and what made me happy. I had become emotionally withdrawn from him and I didn't know how to re-connect.

Whilst his comments were blunt and borne out of frustration and anger at a situation he had no control over, they were painfully accurate. After that conversation I knew something had to change dramatically, but I didn't know where to start.

The personal and grief counselling I pursued after Rachael's death had not been able to assuage the pain, all the self- help books I read had not brought much comfort, and I was relying on anti-depressant medication just to keep my head above water.

I felt completely overwhelmed and had no idea where to begin, but my husband's comment was the catalyst I needed to start my search for happiness.

In hindsight, it was at that moment, the moment when I made the conscious decision to start looking for solutions, that things began to shift for me.

I had set the intention for change and for improvement in the quality of my life. Without realising the magnitude of it at the time, I was embarking on a spiritual journey that would alter my life irrevocably.

Slowly I received and followed intuitive hunches until I found my mentor, Barbara Andrews. Barbara is an intuitive counsellor and I immediately responded to her extraordinary compassion and skill and I credit her with all I have learned.

Over the course of ten years and many healing sessions, Barbara shared her spiritual philosophy with me and gave me practices which opened doorways for me.

I started to explore the metaphysical world, to read philosophy, to listen to new ideas, to change my self-perception and, over time, I peeled away the layers of sadness and fear that had diminished my capacity for joy.

Life slowly started to make sense for me and I realised that these practices had become my roadmap to happiness. I knew that if they worked for me, they would work for others.

During our first meeting, I told Barbara how unhappy my husband and I were and she said, "Never leave a marriage until you are happy with yourself." It was a golden piece of advice because in hindsight, my husband never wanted anything but my happiness. He would have done anything to make me feel better, to ease my grief but I was so caught up in my own despair and loneliness, that it took a long time to work my way back towards him and accept the support he was offering me.

So often we look to something outside of us to make us happy. We think our boyfriends, girlfriends, husbands, wives or children will make us happy. We think money will do it, we think the perfect job will do it, we think losing weight will do it. We think being beautiful or successful will do it. But none of those things make us happy. Those things can enhance our lives greatly yes, but they are not the source of true and sustainable joy. Real joy is an inside job, only you can give it to yourself.

It is my belief that we can only become truly happy when we really love ourselves – but loving ourselves often goes against everything we are taught. When we were growing up, if we valued ourselves we were considered arrogant, up ourselves, pumped. So self-deprecation becomes part of our unconscious behaviour.

When I look at people who are truly happy with their lives, they are all really happy in their own skin. They like themselves, they look after and value themselves.

So how on earth do we get to the place where we like ourselves?

The practices in this book lead the way. They take time and they take commitment, but if you follow them diligently, you'll find them very effective and within six months, you'll notice change in your life.

Some of the steps sound very simple – and they are. But just because they're simple doesn't mean they are easy. They take concerted, conscious daily practice to bring about the change you are seeking.

These practices don't need to be followed in any particular order. Certain ones will resonate immediately and these are the techniques to begin with. They may also be practiced concurrently because, as we all know, life doesn't happen in a tidy, simple format!

This roadmap to happiness will assist you in coming to really know yourself – not the roles you identify with such as wife, husband, mother, father, daughter, son, office worker, painter or whatever your job may be, but an intimate knowledge of your true essence, what motivates you and what your belief systems are.

Once you have this information, you can start to make the changes that bring joy into your life.

So, let's begin!

2

SET THE INTENTION

I remember once hearing Oprah talking about the power of intentions. The interview was years ago and at the time, I didn't really dwell on her words yet they remained in the background of my consciousness, waiting quietly for me to pay attention. This happened when I started reading the Abraham-Hicks material (www.abraham-hicks.com) and I grew to understand the impact that intentions can have on our lives, if we will only take the time to make them.

An intention is defined as 'the act or attitude of determining mentally upon some action or result'.

If we're serious about creating more joy, more abundance, more balance, more peace in our lives – the first thing we need to do is set the intention for it. Intentions breathe life into our desires; they create the foundation upon which we build the life we want.

We need to be very clear with what we want, and create a statement or mantra that captures our intention very clearly.

I have long term and short term intentions that I regularly repeat to myself. I type them up and tape them on to my laptop and my desk.

I write them as I journal and I speak them aloud when I'm out walking by myself.

I repeat them in my meditations and reflect on them throughout the day. Once our intentions have been set, we then need to follow our intuition and universal guidance which will present as synchronicities or symbols, opportunities or advice which we can act upon.

If you're not familiar with the concept of listening to the universe, or adept at reading universal signals and synchronicities, just search Google for one of the many available articles on the topic and find the ones that resonate most with you.

I personally found 'Conversations with the Universe' by Simran Singh a helpful reference tool. It offers detailed insights into how to recognise and interpret guidance when it is presented to us through our dreams, our bodies, our homes, numerology, and other channels.

Once we've set our intention, then we need to trust that what we want will occur – having faith that our intention will become reality is the hard part as change can happen rapidly or slowly and we need to trust universal timing.

Some time ago, I set the intention to identify the underlying cause of the anxiety I have experienced since childhood. A few weeks later, I was told about a new healing tool that can clear trauma from our bodies.

I followed my intuition and made an appointment. I found the sessions on the crystal table very relaxing and whilst there were no immediate epiphanies, it did trigger a series of events and synchronicities that I intuitively knew were linked to the session on the table, and over the course of a couple of months, I was led to the original source of my anxiety. I can now do the inner work required to clear it from my life permanently.

This leads me to the second part of any intention – always make your intention and then request it be given to you with ease and grace. I forgot to ask that the source of my anxiety be shown to me with ease and grace and so whilst the sovereignty table gave me exactly what I asked for, it has also caused huge upheaval in my life.

Through the law of attraction (that energy follows thought), we are always given what we ask for and if we omit the 'ease and grace' aspect, we can be given what we are seeking but not necessarily in the form we are expecting – like me with the table.

I was given the knowledge I was seeking but it was devastating. Had I asked to be given this knowledge with ease and grace, I may have enjoyed an easier integration of the awareness.

Every day upon waking or as we are preparing for the day ahead, it's worthwhile setting the intention for whatever it is that we are seeking – that our day will be productive and joyful, that we will enjoy good health, that we feel loved and valued, that we be given valuable insights or solutions.

Whatever our intention may be, set it and ask that it be received with ease and grace. We then simply remain open to the universal support and signals which present themselves through synchronicities, through nature and the animal world and our own intuition.

Once we start setting intentions and listening to the messages and insights that will start to present themselves, our daily experiences become infinitely richer. Not only do we start to see our intentions become our reality, we enjoy little moments of wonder and delight as we connect more deeply with the world around us.

Our sense of belonging to a family, a community and the world at large is an integral part of our well-being. Coming to appreciate that we are a vital element of this vibrant, dynamic earth and that we are capable of communication on so many levels, is a truly humbling and joyful experience. The world will willingly respond to our intentions if only we will listen and accept the support she offers.

3

FIND TWENTY MINUTES FOR YOURSELF DAILY

When you take time to cultivate a relationship with yourself and learn to love your own company, you will begin to notice small daily wonders that make life lovely. -Unknown

It's easy to feel good and happy when things are going our way, or when we have the time and space for relaxation or spiritual practices that support us.

But what happens when life isn't flowing and relatively easy? This is when we need to make time to build skill sets and practices that balance us so we can accommodate whatever comes our way.

Mastery is when we can feel good regardless of what is happening in our outside world. It means feeling good even when we are frantically busy. It means maintaining our inner balance even when those closest to us are upset. It means feeling centred even if we are in the midst of conflict.

Mastery opens the door to joy and it takes practice, it takes conscious effort. Mastery requires discipline and it requires a degree of solitude.

It requires time, every day, to make a genuine connection with our inner selves, to take the time to listen to the whisperings of our hearts – because our hearts always know what we need, they know what is causing us distress, they know when we're not in our integrity, they know when we're on the wrong path – and we can miss these whisperings if we don't create the space to listen quietly and regularly.

The practice of finding at least twenty minutes daily is vital if we wish to understand our inner world – to reflect on what is going well in our lives and practising gratitude for it – and reflecting on what is not working for us and then doing the inner work to resolve it.

We all need this time to consciously allow ourselves to just be, to allow our feelings to bubble up to the surface. Eckhart Tolle describes it as connecting with our own presence, our essence. Nothing is more important. Nothing will reap bigger dividends. Yet we all find ways to procrastinate. We all find activities to keep us busy, rather than spend 20 to 30 minutes daily in quiet self-reflection and internally oriented activities such as journaling or meditation that create self- awareness.

Self-awareness is vital for genuine happiness. And giving yourself time to develop it is an expression of self-love, a way of valuing yourself, of caring for yourself, of recognising the importance of your own needs.

If this is a new concept for you, read this quick blog by Becky Burton for Holstee.com at www.holstee.com/blogs/mindful-matter/73474117-sunshine-and-snowfall

We live in such a busy, connected world and it's easy to get caught up in everything we 'should' be doing – working, looking after our families, entertaining, exercising, cleaning, shopping, googling.

Yet if we want to create and sustain genuine change in our lives and increase our levels of joy, it's essential to find some quiet time for ourselves daily, doing something that nourishes and balances us. If need be, get up 20 minutes earlier or go to bed 20 minutes later, or sit quietly somewhere for 20 minutes at lunch time.

Spend time in meditation which is great for bringing us in to balance and giving us "Aha!" moments. If meditation is not something you've practiced before, or you're not sure where to begin, there is a fantastic App called 'Headspace'. It starts off with just ten minutes a day of guided meditation and if you choose to continue, it's something like $6 a month. There is a myriad of meditation techniques on line, just choose the one that works best for you. There's no right or wrong, just follow whatever resonates with you the most. Again, meditation takes time and practice but the results are worth it.

If your mind is too busy to meditate, just sit and be totally present with whatever you're feeling – without judgement.

Do something that soothes you – take a salt bath for 20 minutes, sit in nature for 20 minutes with your shoes off, go for a mindful walk, listen to some gentle music, read some philosophy or look through a beautiful book.

Do something that you love – write, sing, play music, draw, garden.

Spend time dreaming. Our imagination is the gateway to manifesting our desires. Energy follows thought and if we can imagine it, we can create it. So start imagining how your dream job feels, visualise your dream home, where is your dream holiday destination, what does your dream partner look like, what do your friendships look like?

Manifesting takes time and 20 minutes daily to spend time picturing your dream life is a great investment.

Find Twenty Minutes For Yourself Daily

If you're not sure where and how to start creating a better life for yourself, visit www.youtube.com/watch?v=8-7Zs-XALDM to get the ball rolling.

There are also many books on the law of attraction and I have found Ester Hicks and Abraham (www.abraham-hicks.com) to be particularly accessible and practical.

Abraham's message is simple but powerful – create and hold the vision of your dream life, feel gratitude for it, and trust it will happen for you.

I used to find this practice challenging as my belief systems set limits on what I thought I could achieve but I persisted. It has taken me ten years but I now know that anything is possible. If we imagine it, hold the vision and trust, then we just have to follow our intuition and universal guidance and it will manifest – easier said than done but it works – it just takes time and practice.

If you're having a great day and feeling extremely pleased about something, just spend your 20 minutes sitting in gratitude – it's the best way to enhance joy in your life.

If you're feeling flat, do some journaling for 20 minutes as free writing often helps identify the source of any disturbance. It doesn't matter what you do with the 20 minutes, what is important is that you give yourself that time every day to do something that nourishes, comforts or inspires you.

Self-love, self-appreciation, self-care – all of these are integral to increasing joy in our lives. As I mentioned earlier, happy people have a healthy appreciation of themselves, they care for themselves and make their needs a priority.

Finding time every day to make a genuine connection with ourselves is an expression of this self-love. Like any relationship, our relationship to ourselves needs to be nurtured and supported, and 20 minutes daily is an invaluable way of building the foundations for what you want for your life.

If you don't yet know what makes you happy, or why you may be unhappy, spend some time getting to know yourself – take a Myers Briggs test to determine your personality type, strengths and weaknesses (www.personalitypage.com). Take an enneagram test to find out what makes you tick (www.enneagraminstitute.com).

Self-knowledge is powerful, it gives you insights in to what will make you happy and how to honour your personal needs – I learned this the hard way!

I had no idea why I wasn't thriving in a social job that most people would love until I took the Myers Briggs test. I was surprised to find that I am an introvert and since making sure that I now have two days working from home, in complete solitude, I am a much happier person.

I was also really surprised to find out that I'm much more creative than I gave myself credit for. Because I am a highly organised and efficient person I had always chosen account management or operational roles and yet I am much happier spending two days a week researching and writing.

As you do this growth work and begin to start caring for yourself, and hopefully putting yourself first, you may notice that some of your friends/ family/ colleagues resist the changes you are making. If you have been a person that always puts others first or allows others to treat you in a less than respectful way, you may find yourself unwilling to tolerate these behaviours any longer.

Just observe your reactions and take the time to decide how you wish to respond. If the relationship was not based on a mutual respect and love, it may be time to allow it to dissolve.

Peggy Black, a medium who channels 'The Team', constantly teaches us that we are the creators of our lives and yet not many of us have been lucky enough to have been taught this – I know I wasn't. I grew up thinking life just happened to me, I didn't realise I was an active participant in how my life turned out.

Peggy encourages us to tap in to our imagination because it is our most powerful 'creator/ive tool'. So start imagining your dream job, your dream home, your dream relationships and lifestyle – it's fun and it's such a productive way to pass time.

And the moment you allow yourself to 'become' your imagination, you have entered what Abraham of 'The Law of Attraction' calls 'the vortex', the place where all you ever want is waiting for you.

As an adult it may feel strange playing imagination games and yet I really believe that it's where creation of a new and better life begins. You need to have the vision before you can become it.

And once you have identified the life you want, the experiences you want, the relationships you want, the health you want, then you can start using practices to bring it in to being.

So remember, 20 minutes for yourself daily is vital for joy. You can't know what makes your soul happy if you don't create space to listen to it!

4

THE WORLD IS OUR MIRROR

"A loving person lives in a loving world. A hostile person lives in a hostile world. Everyone you meet is your mirror," says Ken Keyes Junior in the 'Handbook of Higher Consciousness'.

I remember when my teacher, Barbara, first said to me: "The world is your mirror," how much I resisted that statement. There are so many awful things happening in the world today, people hurting each other, betraying each other, not respecting each other and I didn't like being associated with such negative behaviour.

"I don't think I treat people poorly," I said, quietly affronted.

"You may not do it to others," Barb said, "but you do it to yourself. Whenever we have an emotional reaction to someone's behaviour or a situation around us, it is a strong indicator that we may be treating ourselves the same way." I couldn't argue with that one.

I started paying attention to the day-to-day experiences that disturbed me in any way. I would identify the underlying behaviours that distressed me and ask myself how I was treating myself in the same way.

When clients weren't valuing my time and services, I could see that I wasn't valuing my personal time, that I was wasting it on activities that didn't serve me.

If I witnessed a disrespectful interaction I would look for where I wasn't respecting my own self – through poor diet, putting myself down, allowing myself to be taken for granted.

If I was let down by people, I would look for where I was letting myself down and often it was through judgemental behaviour. I used to be very judgemental of greedy or tight fisted people, thinking they didn't have enough generosity of spirit to share. I have since learned that all negative behaviours are fear based and I have no right to judge anyone's behaviour except my own.

I find this mirror technique especially helpful when I'm having an intense reaction to someone else's feelings. Until recently, I used to feel anxious being around anyone who was really angry or deeply distressed but I now understand that whenever I'm struggling to tolerate someone else's feelings, it's often because I find it hard to tolerate those feelings in myself.

The reason I found it so hard to witness someone else's rage was because I was scared of my own intense anger. At times I have felt overwhelmed by an indescribable fury that terrified me and so I did anything I could to push it down, to ignore it. I did such a good job of denying this rage that I forgot the origin of it (thereby losing my chance to resolve it) and I developed chronic anxiety and phobias.

It was the same when someone I loved was in pain. I couldn't bear to see them distressed and vulnerable because it mirrored my own deeply buried pain.

This is where using the mirror is an invaluable tool for showing us what areas of ourselves we need to work on and heal.

Once I realised that the anger and pain I found so hard to witness in others was a reflection of my own grief and rage, I asked my Divine self, my God self, to show me the origin of these deeply buried feelings.

It took two years and I needed expert guidance at times, but I finally realised where these terrible feelings came from. I could acknowledge the feelings and their origins and then start the healing process.

So, if we are witnessing or experiencing poor behaviour from others and we are reacting to it, it is often an indication we are treating ourselves this way, or we have felt or have been treated this way before.

The next step is to then ask our Higher Selves (our Spirit, our Divine Intelligence, or God or Source energy – whoever we trust to be the source of all knowledge) to show us when we have felt this way before. It can help to ask these questions in meditation or prayer. I often ask the question when I'm going for a long walk or sitting quietly, as I know that if I create and allow the space, the answer will be given to me.

Please bear in mind that sometimes the answers we receive can be confronting or painful. When we ask to be shown the origin of any negative feeling, it helps to have an open mind and to be prepared to look at whatever arises with honesty and with compassion for ourselves.

I had a client whose buttons were being pushed by the way her five year old granddaughter was being neglected by her parents. She recognised the child was in need of greater physical attention.

Using the mirror as a tool, I asked my client to consider what had happened to her when she was five. How had she been neglected in some way and within moments, she immediately recalled a deeply buried memory of being sexually abused at five years of age. The moment she recalled this trauma, she recognised it as the trigger point for her current disturbance and she could then start the healing required.

Whilst this was an unusually quick and spontaneous recollection of past trauma, it is an indication of the information that is available to us when we are open to the messages our world presents us with – it tells us where we are out of alignment, what needs our attention.

Once we have done the healing work around a particular issue, we no longer need the world to keep reflecting it to us. If the world keeps presenting us with the same image or message, albeit in a different way each time, it means we have more clearing work to do.

The world also mirrors our belief systems. I remember sitting in a business meeting and our client acknowledged how successful and profitable our campaign had been for him but "We don't really care about the idea, we want more revenue so we want you to cut your margin."

I was full of indignation at his lack of regard for our efforts and it took me a good few hours to calm down and recognise it was his inference that 'you don't matter' that infuriated me so much. Once I got in touch with this feeling, I realised I have long held the belief system that my feelings were irrelevant and that I had to defer to those who were more powerful, or who had more authority than I did.

While I know intellectually that this is not correct, our client's comments definitely pushed the buttons of my inner child who had been very passive and felt this way on countless occasions, and so I now needed to do the clearing work around that belief system (see Chapter Nine for assistance).

Hopefully now that I have recognised this belief system, and now honour my inner child and assert myself when necessary, I will not need the world to keep reflecting this message to me – I have well and truly received it!

Equally, the world is also our mirror whenever we are inspired by the beauty, joy, kindness or love we are witnessing in any given moment. In this case the world is reflecting our own inner beauty back to us.

The world around us is an invaluable guidance tool and the universe will do anything it can to bring our attention to any personal issues that require addressing. If our life is going smoothly, our relationships with others are thriving and we are genuinely not having an emotional response to any negative behaviours or situations around us, then we know we are balanced and in alignment with the Divine, with our Higher Selves.

If we are reacting to a distressing situation or an uncomfortable interaction, it is serving its purpose as our mirror and letting us know we have growth work to do. We need to identify the offending behaviour and ask how we are treating ourselves, or others, this way and then address it.

Once we have done the processing or healing work required of us, we experience greater personal freedom and joy.

5

THE IMPORTANCE OF REFRAMING

Joyful people are always reframing their position; they are constantly making the choice to look up and out rather than down and in. It sounds very simple but reframing takes awareness and practice to bring about the change we are seeking.

If reframing is not something you've done a lot of, it can be helpful to choose a topic every day and write a half page about the positive aspects of it. It can be any topic, it doesn't matter; you just have to consider what's good about it.

You don't have to spend a lot of time on it, five minutes every morning or every night before bed is enough to start training your mind to look for the positive rather than the negative in any situation. Doing this starts laying the new neural pathways that will lead you to a more contented state of mind.

In 2013 I was unwell and spent most of my time in bed or hospital but it was an amazing year in terms of personal growth. I was able to meditate often, I was able to read and practice all of the spiritual philosophies Barbara, my mentor, had been teaching me for the past six years. It was a magical time of change for me, I really learned what being 'conscious' meant and I knew this was the way I wanted to live.

Then I recovered and re-entered the workforce full time. Life returned to its usual frantic pace which was a major shock to my system, and I found it really hard to stick to the spiritual practices I'd been taught.

It was easy to stay centred and balanced when I was sick at home and protected from the daily interactions and demands of work. It was easy to hold the vision of what I wanted for myself when I had the time to meditate, to practice gratitude and keep myself focused on the positive aspects of my life. It was easy to clear any anger or pain that arose when I had the time to sit with these feelings and allow them to pass.

However it was a different ball game once I was back at work. I found myself dreading interaction with tricky clients and the myriad of challenges that arose daily.

It was a good nine months before I realised how much time I was spending bemoaning the various aspects of the job and remembered to reframe. For a while I had to reframe several times an hour, until I got to the place where I felt good about being at work.

Rather than whinge about difficult clients, I practised gratitude for the fact they paid. Rather than whinge about working 30 days straight, I practised gratitude that I could generate income. Rather than whinge about the unethical business practices I was encountering, I practised gratitude for the experience I was being given in dealing with injustice.

Every hour of every day until it became second nature, I had to reframe. I had to remember that energy follows thought, I had to consciously focus on the positive aspects of my job.

Leaving work wasn't an option so the only way I could increase my happiness levels was to change my perception of my job, and start practising gratitude for the parts of it that were working for me.

It's not easy to start with but it's the same for all of us. If we're in a job or relationship or situation we don't enjoy but can't change in the immediate future, we need to start visualising and feeling gratitude for our dream job, relationship or whatever it is we would like to have.

In the interim, it's vital to also find things to be grateful for in our current situation – whether it's the fact we're earning an income, that we don't have to work weekends, that our husband doesn't cheat on us, that our wife is a good cook, that we have a comfortable bed, that we have a loving pet, that we have someone to nurse us, that our children are happy, that we're healthy, that we have good friends – whatever it may be, we need to find and focus on something we can appreciate about the life situation we're not enjoying.

Maintaining a base line of joy in our life requires mastery. Mastery is all about taking responsibility for ourselves and our feelings and not allowing ourselves to go in to victim mode – and it takes constant practice! In reframing, we find something to feel grateful for and gratitude is the quickest way to lift our vibration and our mood.

6

DON'T DO ANYTHING THAT DOESN'T LIFT YOUR ENERGY

Often we feel compelled to commit to activities that don't really appeal to us: like host that dinner party when we'd rather have a quiet weekend; attend that coffee date that doesn't really suit; complete that exercise we think we should be doing.

Unless it's a professional or familial responsibility which demands our attention, we don't actually have to DO anything, we always have a choice.

I used to commit to so many functions, committees and charities out of a self-imposed sense of duty that I was run ragged with no time to myself. I felt obliged to do whatever was asked of me because I believed that's what a good friend/wife/mother/ daughter does.

But there is no rule book that says we have to do something because someone else wants us to. We all have a choice.

The decision to partake in an activity is ours alone. So if we can start asking ourselves – does my energy lift at the thought of this activity, or does it fall – and we start listening to the answer, and honouring it, our lives become more pleasurable.

Several years ago one of my spiritual teachers, Grant, told me that my first responsibility is to myself; then to my husband and son; then to my birth family; then the world at large.

At first I resisted his suggestion, feeling it to be a very selfish way of approaching life. Like many of us, I was raised to put other people's needs before my own and be of service wherever I could but over time, I have come to believe that my teacher is right.

We often do whatever is asked of us without first considering if we feel good about it – will you come for dinner? Will you pick up my kids? Will you donate to this charity? Will you drive me here? Will you meet me there?

Every day we are met with requests for our time, our love, our money or our skills, and it takes mindfulness to start taking a moment to consider if our energy rises at the thought of a particular activity.

At times, we begrudgingly commit to engagements because we feel we 'should'. The word 'should' is a red flag we need to pay attention to. It suggests we may be committing to something out of duty rather than desire. If our energy doesn't rise at the thought of participating, then it's in our best interests to graciously decline.

Our decisions may not be popular with our family or friends, but it's more important we honour our own feelings, than capitulate to the pressure of theirs.

We may feel uncomfortable at first, as it takes practice to learn how to say no, but until we start really valuing ourselves enough to put our own needs first, we will experience more resentment than joy in our lives.

If we have a choice, and generally we do, we are always happier when we tune in to our hearts, into what *feels* right for us, rather than what we *think* we should do.

When we start living from our hearts this way, we are being authentic. Life begins to flow with greater ease and our sense of contentment and satisfaction with our lives increases.

Our heart is the physical and emotional power source of our being. To live more joyfully, it's vital that our daily lives are aligned with what our hearts want. We achieve this by allowing our actions to be motivated by our hearts first, and then supported by our minds.

Yet many of us have been raised to make decisions, both major and minor, in a methodical, practical manner, to weigh up the pros and cons and make decisions accordingly. We are conditioned to act from our intellect, from our head space rather than our heart space.

But it is our heart that always knows what is best for us. It is the most reliable navigation tool we will ever have. It will never lead us astray – all we have to do is honour its messages, even though following our hearts can be incredibly difficult at times. It can mean making really hard decisions, and the emotional fallout can be huge before our lives improve.

Living from our hearts takes practice and mindfulness to slow down and listen to them. And then it takes courage, sometimes more courage than we think we possess, to act on their direction.

If we're in a job, a relationship, a life situation that doesn't make our heart energy rise, then it's time to change – or at least put a plan for change into action. This can be terrifying, especially if we have been in an unhealthy relationship or role for an extended period of time. If we're lonely or financially insecure then it's even harder to leave a situation that isn't serving us.

Don't Do Anything That Doesn't Lift Your Energy 39

So how do we heed the messages of our heart when we're immobilised by fear? How do we make positive changes when we're scared and don't know where to start?

We start by *trusting* that a solution is already available to us.

Even though we may not know what it is yet, we have to trust the solution is ready and waiting for us. We then follow our intuition and universal guidance until our solution or required course of action becomes clear to us.

While this may sound implausible or ridiculous, I know it to be the truth. There is always a solution, an answer to any problem, and we will always find it if we listen to and follow the direction of our hearts – it is as simple and as hard as that.

I'll never forget watching the television coverage after the Thailand tsunami and a woman had lost her loved ones, as well as everything she had ever owned. She was overwhelmed with grief and panic and the journalist asked her how she was going to move forward.

The woman stood weeping and thought quietly for a moment, and then she answered, "I'll go where the love is." The reporter looked bewildered and asked for further clarification. "I'll have to rely on the volunteers, these strangers who have willingly come here to help us. I have nothing else so I have to rely on their kindness," replied the woman.

When we need to make huge changes in our lives, particularly painful ones, we have to do the same thing, we have to go to where the love is – to look to those who love us, who will support and encourage us. If need be, we get professional help and if this isn't financially viable, we look to volunteer support groups.

There is always a solution. Even though we may feel alone at times, we are never alone, and we are never without assistance, we just have to be willing to accept it in to our lives.

Until recently, I was working full time in an office but I was professionally unfulfilled and bored with my daily routine. My mind/ego was telling me that I couldn't afford to work part time, that I 'should' be in the office full time to ensure I was completely in control of my part of the business.

I kept reframing my thoughts around my job and I could genuinely appreciate how fortunate I was to be working in a flexible job, in a lovely office close to home, where I was paid well and so I persevered.

However I was only listening to my mind, I completely forgot to listen to my heart. When I actually stopped over the holidays and tuned in to what my heart was saying, it was begging me to make a change.

I was exhausted with the intense demands of managing a business as well as running our home, finances and superannuation, caring for our son and writing a book.

I had grown up believing I had to be in complete control of every facet of my life in order for it to function properly. I also believed that I had to work hard to ensure financial security so this is how I had always operated.

These belief systems weren't serving me and at the end of the day, I realised that if I wanted a happier life, I had to make a choice. I had to let go of these belief systems that were not serving me. I had to stop doing what my ego/mind insisted upon and start listening to what my body/heart was telling me.

My husband made some suggestions to help reduce the pressure I was feeling and he willingly stepped in to take on some household duties, but my ego really struggled with it. My husband now happily makes our son's lunch and does some household chores, yet I still have to resist the temptation to step in and do them quickly rather than allow him to do them in his own time. I now work from home every alternate day and have to trust that office tasks will be fulfilled without my supervision.

These may not sound like major changes but I found them uncomfortable to begin with as I am so used to being in control, it makes me feel safe. However, my frame of mind has improved dramatically and I am much happier with my daily life. My energy definitely rises when I know I will be working the next day from home, and this lift carries me through my days in the office.

Taking time to truly 'feel' into a situation, to whether it feels good, rather than just mentally evaluating it, will often give us a totally different perspective. I believe decisions that *feel* good, rather than those based purely on our intellect, are the most life affirming decisions.

Like many people, there have been times during our marriage when both my husband and I have been fed up with each other and thought that life would be easier separate rather than together.

If ever I find myself in this position, I do some journaling to settle my mind, and empty it of all its judgements and complaints, and then I feel into what my heart is telling me.

The moment I do this I know that I never want to be without him, that it is just my mind creating disturbance, and I can feel myself shift from a critical perspective to one of appreciation. My energy rises at the thought of him as he is the most loyal and generous of men. He has a fine and creative mind which is always open to new ideas, his persistence and enthusiasm are endless and he has the patience of a saint. He never judges or censures others and he is extremely quick to forgive. The moment I drop out of my head and into my heart, I move very quickly to state of deep appreciation for all that he is.

Living from the heart, taking note of what lifts our energy, takes practice and time. It's vital that we create quiet periods daily to really tune in to whatever is happening in our lives as often, our feelings will contradict our thoughts.

When we reflect on our lives and they are flowing easily, we will feel gratitude and lightness. When we are facing obstacles and take time to *feel* into what is right for us, we will always find our answer, the best path for us. It may not be the easiest, but in the long run it will be for our highest good.

When we have the discipline to listen and the courage to follow our hearts this way, we are creating opportunities for more joy in our daily lives.

7

PAY ATTENTION TO EVERY THOUGHT AND WORD

Many of us are familiar with the 'energy follows thought' concept. Scientists have now proven that when we focus our attention on an object we can alter its behaviour, down to the sub-atomic particle level.

That means that every thought and word we say and think has a vibration – a positive or negative charge that becomes stronger with repetition. Therefore, when we think negatively about ourselves and say we're fat, we're unsuccessful, we're lonely, we're unattractive, we've got no money – we are strengthening a pattern which makes it harder to break.

Creating more joy in our lives means paying attention to how we think and talk about ourselves, and catching ourselves every time we think a negative thought or utter a negative word about ourselves – even the impulsive ones like when someone tells us we look lovely and our first response is to say, "No, I don't!" Start accepting compliments even if you feel like a fraud.

It really is a case of fake it until you make it – until your perception of yourself moves from one of criticism to one of appreciation and kindness to yourself. When I first started this practice I began by looking in the mirror several times a day and saying to my reflection, "I am beautiful. I am precious. I am love." At first I felt ridiculous and embarrassed but over a period of time, talking to myself in a gentle and loving manner began to build a sense of self-worth that was lacking as a child and younger woman.

When starting out, put little red dots about your house, on the mirror, on your steering wheel, to remind you to start saying positive things about yourself – I am fulfilled, I am successful, I am love, I am creativity, I am courageous, I am emotionally balanced, I am healthy, I am in a job I love, I am fit, I am slim, I am peaceful, I am abundantly wealthy.

The constant repetition of positive "I AM" statements is far more powerful than it sounds. Our 'I Am' presence is our spiritual identity, our Higher Self that is connected to Source, to God. These positive I AM statements align our human will with our Divine self, to the God within that can do or be anything.

Repeating these statements with intention and gratitude strengthens their vibration so it's impossible for them not to occur – it's simply the Law of Attraction.

Many of you may be familiar with Jerry and Esther Hicks who channel the spiritual entity known as 'Abraham' (www.abraham-hicks.com). Abraham is the spiritual consciousness that discusses the law of attraction and its many implications. Over and over again, Abraham repeats the same message – that what we focus on is what we create in our lives. If we focus on lack then we will experience lack in our lives. If we focus on abundance, then we will experience abundance in our lives.

If we are constantly worrying about our poor finances, we can often find ourselves short. If we focus on our poor health we will attract more of the same. If we focus on our bad relationships, again we create discord rather than harmony.

But! If we allow ourselves to start thinking about what it is we really want for ourselves and our lives, if we start visualising it and – most importantly – feeling gratitude for it, enjoying the feeling of having it even though it hasn't yet arrived, then it will start to materialise in our lives.

See yourself thriving, see yourself as successful, see yourself in a wonderful relationship, see yourself

Energy follows thought so what we focus on is what we create in our lives.

Making positive I AM statements about ourselves and holding the vision of what we want brings about the changes we desire.

fulfilled and happy in retirement, see your career flying, see yourself as peaceful and present.

Don't worry or get caught up in how it will happen because that part will take care of itself. Our job is just to visualise or feel what it is that we want for ourselves and to feel gratitude for it. Once we start doing this on a regular basis, we will start to notice ways and means of achieving our goals – someone will say something that triggers a solution or an opportunity will present itself, a person will appear out of left field to help facilitate our goal. I realise this may sound impossible to many readers but it works!

All we have to do is hold the vision and follow the opportunities and intuitive hunches that will present themselves in our lives. Universal guidance will lead the way.

Holding a vision and an attitude of gratitude is demanding. It requires we be present and constantly aware of our thoughts and feelings about ourselves.

If you notice that you are consistently saying or thinking a particularly negative thing about yourself, it may be helpful to do a cut from that belief (see Chapter Nine).

If you need practice in how to raise your energetic vibration and hold the vision of what you want, go to www.abraham-hicks.com and watch some of the quick videos that are free. You don't have to spend a lot of time, five minutes every few days is enough to remind you of how to create your vision and how to hold it.

If you need practice in personal confidence, Google the terrific TED talk by Amy Cuddy. Cuddy is a Harvard University researcher and she talks of body language and the powerful physiological impact that certain physical poses can have on us. It's a technique I often rely on when going in to meetings, pitches or potentially confrontational situations and it has had a dramatic impact on my self-esteem. I no longer feel like a vulnerable or hesitant participant but a confident and capable woman, and it makes a huge difference to how I am received.

For further insight on how our words and thoughts can alter our lives, there's a great video at Oprah.com by Pastor Joel Osteen on how words can determine your destiny.

It takes practice to start with but being vigilant with our thoughts and feelings about ourselves has a huge impact on the quality of our lives.

8

FIND YOUR PASSION

Ten years ago I read the headline "Live your passion!"

My immediate thought was that I didn't have any passions. Even though I was 38, I had never cultivated any hobbies or creative pursuits that I loved and I had no idea where to begin.

My teacher, Barbara Andrews, suggested I read 'The Artist's Way' by Julia Cameron which was great advice. The Artist's Way is a 12 week exercise that leads the reader away from practical left brain activity and into creative right brain activity in a simple and effective manner.

Some aspects of the book are a bit confronting as they require some self-analysis which can be a little uncomfortable. Our inner saboteur will also always find a way of convincing us that we're no good at something, but it's worth persisting with the book.

Through The Artist's Way, I figured out that I love to write. As words flow onto the pages of my daily journal, I feel emptied of the emotion I feel building up internally. It dissipates feelings of anger and anxiety and it helps me clarify situations – I feel lighter when I'm finished journaling. It's also a wonderfully creative pursuit. When I've written a great phrase or sentence, I feel really contented and happy with my efforts.

I realised I love gardening. I find it peaceful and relaxing when I weed, feed, trim and talk to my plants. Every time I look out on the garden I feel great appreciation for its beauty and a sense of satisfaction that I created it from nothing.

I discovered I love visiting interior design stores. I find real pleasure in looking at beautiful things, it makes me feel happy when I look at skilled craftsmanship and see someone's creative vision in physical form.

If you're considering pursuing a creative passion but feeling anxious about your ability or skill, then I highly recommend listening to Brene Brown in one of her TED talks https://blog.ted.com/vulnerability-is-the-birthplace-of-innovation-creativity-and-change-brene-brown-at-ted2012/. Brown studies vulnerability, courage, authenticity and shame and she rightly claims that unless your critics are also daring to be authentic and vulnerable, they're not worth listening to.

What matters is that you give yourself opportunities to immerse yourself in a creative process purely for the pleasure it brings, rather than worrying about the end result. It doesn't matter if the painting or writing or song is no good, it matters that you gave yourself the freedom to express yourself creatively.

Creative expression takes courage. When we're trying new things, sometimes we'll do a great job and sometimes we'll miss the mark entirely. It's no big deal, we just need to pick ourselves up and try again.

I learned the hard way that it doesn't matter what anyone else thinks of our creative efforts. I remember completing my first piece of writing eight years ago and I was really excited about it so I showed it to Simon, my husband. His first reaction was: "Ugh, that's far too flowery for me, not my go at all."

I was mortified. I felt so embarrassed and ashamed of my efforts that I didn't write again for years, which was such a waste of time yet I can't blame anyone but myself for that.

Ironically, it was also Simon who got me writing again by encouraging me to write the blogs for our business website. He suggested I write in a more personal style than I was used to, and in doing so he opened up a whole new world for me.

Writing is now one of the joys of my life where I write authentically, rather than trying to write for an audience which I found inhibiting.

At the end of the day, it doesn't matter what anyone else thinks of what we create, the only thing that matters is how much satisfaction *we* get from the process.

As Oprah says in an interview on courage with Brene Brown, failure isn't bad or wrong or an indication of our worth, it's simply "there to inform us to move in a different direction."

Oprah is arguably one of the most successful, competent women in the world but she still has her vulnerabilities and challenges, her successes and failures. We all do, it is part of the human condition.

When we can put fear of failure or self-criticism aside, and give ourselves the time and opportunity to immerse ourselves in a creative process, it can bring enormous satisfaction.

My son is an amateur painter and I marvel at his ability to sketch and paint with abandon. He doesn't care if his strokes aren't perfect, he doesn't care if the end result isn't a masterpiece; he just loves getting lost in the moment. He enjoys seeing his vision come to life on the canvas and he intuitively knows that the only thing that matters is that he is enjoying himself. Children are great teachers this way. They surrender to the creative process which enhances their sense of personal satisfaction and pleasure in any given moment.

My husband is a talented guitarist and songwriter and the moment he picks up a guitar, the creative process transports him into a whole different space where the pressures of daily life fall away from him. He is also an amazing stage performer. Even now, every time I watch him at a gig, I am mesmerised by his talent and charisma and I forget the hours he has devoted to practice. He has been inexorably enthusiastic and persistent and it has translated into a passion that sustains him through everything life serves up.

As we get older and commence secondary and tertiary education, we tend to focus on left brain logic and reason which is an integral part of academic competence.

However, developing right brain thinking is just as crucial as it encourages imagination, problem solving and intuition.

If we don't get this balance right and our left brain thinking becomes dominant, it can stifle our creativity which is how we explore our imagination, our intuition and ultimately our full potential.

To enhance right brain thinking – and our creative potential – there are simple exercises we can do – just visit Google for right brain exercises. With time, these exercises increase our creative thinking and imagination which opens doors for us.

Inspiring, stimulating hobbies can be found in books, magazines and newspapers, council activities, through mentors, through trial and error – simply trying something and seeing if it feels good. The time and energy we spend in finding a passion rewards us time and again. Set the intention to find your passion and see what presents itself!

Creative pursuits give our souls the chance to speak, to be seen and heard. When we are creatively engaged, we are exploring our unique potential, the aspect of ourselves that we alone can bring to the world.

When we're creatively engaged, we're being led by our hearts rather than our minds and our energetic vibration expands. Our energy and mood lifts and when our vibration is high, life flows with greater ease.

Creative expression is a basic stepping stone to joy. When creating, we are being proactive with our lives, rather than reactive. It increases our sense of fulfilment, of satisfaction with ourselves and our lives.

It creates opportunities for joy to bubble up and be experienced.

9

EVALUATE BELIEF SYSTEMS

What are belief systems? Belief systems are the precepts we live by, a collection of thoughts and actions that we practise and repeat so often they become beliefs and habits that shape our behaviour. As such, our belief systems become the foundation of our life experience.

We are not born with belief systems. We learn them unconsciously from our parents, our siblings, our teachers, our friends, our culture, our religion and the media. We assume that because we have been raised with them, that they are correct but that is not necessarily the case. Many of our belief systems can be inhibiting or negative and they obstruct our capacity for joy.

We all have numerous belief systems and a necessary step for increasing our happiness is to identify our belief systems and get rid of the ones that don't serve us.

For example, some people have the belief system that money is hard to come by. Knowing that energy follows thought, this is not a helpful belief system to live with. If you believe money is hard to earn, that's how you'll experience it.

Other people have the belief system that you have to be thin to be beautiful. It means we feel miserable about ourselves if we are not supermodel thin. I know from personal experience this is an exhausting belief system to live with. I spent years in my twenties and thirties limiting my calorie intake so I could be thin and any time I tipped the scales at more than 54 kilos, I felt terrible for the entire day, week or month that I perceived myself to be overweight. It was a tremendous waste of time and energy and I missed countless opportunities to be happy because I was so fixated on my weight. Yet it wasn't until I started evaluating my belief systems that I realised I was so attached to the belief that I had to be thin to be lovable. After doing the inner work to change this belief system, I now allow myself to enjoy food and I have put on weight but I still have to be careful not to slip back into this old pattern.

Others yet believe they have to be perfect. They try to be the perfect wife, the perfect son, the perfect colleague, the perfect hostess, the perfect friend which is another exhausting belief system to live with because it means we're looking outside of ourselves for validation and appreciation, and we can feel devastated if we fall short of others, or our own expectations! When we're trying to be perfect, we're not being our authentic selves, which is where we will find joy.

Some people believe life should be fair so they spend a great deal of time bemoaning the injustices done to them rather than accepting what is and doing what they can to change their own immediate circumstances and accepting what they can't change.

Others believe that everyone else's needs are more important than their own so they spend their lives looking after other people rather than themselves. If we deny ourselves and our own yearnings for an extended period of time, our bodies will find a way of waking us up and drawing our attention to the imbalance in our lives.

We all have our own set of conditionings or beliefs that limit us in some way.

When I was a child, I formed the belief that I had to be a 'good girl', agreeable to all those around me in order to be safe and accepted. I was a very acquiescent child and teenager, often to my own detriment. During the first twenty years of our marriage, I generally accepted everything my husband said and did, even when I didn't agree with him, because I didn't want to upset or displease him in any way.

Over time I became resentful and started thinking it was his fault that I was so miserable. But I couldn't blame anyone else for this situation as I had created it myself with my own belief that I had to be a 'good girl' and accept whatever anyone said or did, and so it was up to me to make the changes.

Much as the changes I've made are much healthier for me personally, my husband says that his life was much easier during our first twenty years together and he is right! Changing fundamental belief systems isn't easy and it will affect the dynamics of the most important relationships in our lives.

While part of my husband is joking, I know part of him also misses the acquiescent woman I used to be and I can still feel a bit anxious that the changes I have made may jeopardise our relationship in some way. However, it is a risk I'm prepared to take in order to live a happier, healthier life.

The difficulty with belief systems is that is we don't even realise how powerful they are until we start to really evaluate them and then change them.

To identify unhealthy belief systems, we need to start paying attention to our thoughts and conversations –

whenever we hear ourselves saying 'can't' or 'should', it's an indication there may be a belief system that needs changing. Start listening to yourself and whenever you hear yourself saying something negative, look to the belief system behind it and if it's limiting you in some way, get rid of it.

So, how do we change a belief system? There are several ways and you need to find the one that works best for you personally.

For me, the most powerful tool is Phyllis Krystal's 'Cutting the ties that bind' method (https://www.phylliskrystal.com/). As Krystal says on her website and in her book of the same name, this method of 'cutting' from negative belief systems is not a quick fix, it takes dedication and time but it works.

Her method involves identifying a belief system that doesn't serve us and doing a quick daily practice for two weeks to 'cut' from it. Sometimes it may even take three or four weeks if it's a deeply entrenched belief system.

For that two week period, we spend eight minutes a day doing a visual exercise where our belief system is in the top of a gold figure 8, we are in the bottom of the golden figure 8 and we mentally trace a blue light around the figure 8, mentally separating the two circles with the blue colour of Divine will. At the end of the two week period, we are led through a finishing process which takes up to an hour with a three day integration period.

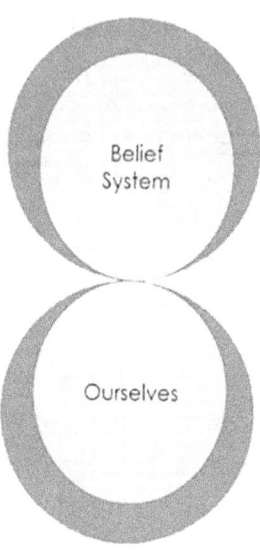

As I'm a person that finds it hard to concentrate on a mental image, I find it helpful to get a piece of paper and draw in the golden circles, write in the belief system I am cutting from and then trace the golden figure eight with a blue pen four times a day.

It sounds time consuming and it is, but it's a very powerful process and it impacts on both our physical and emotional bodies. We often dream heavily, we can come down with a physical ailment or we can feel miserable or flat, depending on the cut.

Each cut will be experienced differently, depending on how deeply we are attached to it. I often get sick before or during a cut, I can feel very angry or upset and I dream vividly – so make sure to choose your timing well when you're doing one!

Don't start a cut before an important event or during a time you won't have the freedom to allow your reactions to surface. It's also good to let those you're close to know when you're doing a cut as they'll be impacted by it if you're more emotional than usual.

The best cuts to start with are individual cuts from your mother and father because we subconsciously take on so many of our parents' values and beliefs. We don't cut from their positive aspects, just the unhelpful beliefs we have absorbed from them.

To determine if a belief system is a positive or negative one for you (and they are all subjective), we simply ask ourselves during a quiet time of contemplation if the behaviours and responses it asks of us are life enhancing or not. I find if I really feel into the question that I get an intuitive response. Again, when we find ourselves saying 'can't' or 'should', it's an indication that we need to look a little deeper at the belief system behind our behaviour and ask if it's really serving us.

For example, I grew up believing that 'Life is ordinary', that it was a slog, something to be got through rather than enjoyed.

But once I started doing this cutting work, I realised that this belief wasn't at all true for me. For me, life is an extraordinary and precious experience. There are heartbreaking times and there are exhilarating times. There are devastating times and there are uplifting times and I value them all. I now truly appreciate that the world, including me, is full of contrast – full of great despair and great hope, great sadness and great joy and it is my job to embrace the fullness of it all, to welcome the diversity for the amazing moments and opportunities it offers me. This contrast tells me when I have personal growth work to do and deepens my appreciation for the wonderful times.

Once I understood the impact of belief systems on my daily life, I realised I could change my own reality if I was prepared to do the work. So I started evaluating the belief systems I had grown up with and cutting from belief systems that didn't enhance my life.

I thought I would find the cut from my mother far more intense than the cut from my father and yet the reverse was true. I had obviously absorbed a lot more of my father's patterning than I realised and you may find the same true for yourself.

I realised I carried my father's anxiety regarding money and so I cut from the belief that I needed financial security to be happy and safe. It was very fortunate I did that cut because straight afterwards, our business was dramatically affected by the digital disruption and my husband and I went through a very financially difficult period for two years, but I actually managed relatively well because I'd done the cut.

During that time, I started spending a lot of time in nature which calmed my nervous system and I also nurtured my interest in the metaphysical world and my own spirituality which has become the focus of my life. Apart from family, it is my greatest source of joy and I spend countless hours immersed in this pursuit. There is so much to be learned from other people's hard earned wisdom which is readily available on the internet. Had I not done the cut from my fear of financial destitution, these two years would have been an extremely traumatic period rather than a relatively peaceful time of personal growth.

After cutting from negative beliefs adopted from our parents, it is helpful to start asking ourselves what belief systems or people we are living with that limit our potential for joy.

Is there someone in your life creating disturbance, anger or sadness, such as an ex husband or wife, girlfriend or boyfriend, who you need to cut from? The only people you can't cut with are those you are in a current sexual relationship with, and any children under the age of 15.

After cutting from your parents and those in your life who are causing you distress, start asking yourself what beliefs inhibit your confidence or freedom.

If you're not sure where to start, do a meditation or start journaling daily. Ask your Higher Self to show you the limiting thoughts or beliefs that you are ready to eliminate from your life.

If meditation isn't your thing, take notice of the occasions during your day where you feel out of balance or agitated and ask yourself what belief system is behind it – if it's a belief that doesn't serve you, do a cut or look to the internet for other methods of clearing negative beliefs.

Gary van Warmerdam has a wonderful book – 'MindWorks: A Practical Guide for Changing Thoughts, Beliefs and Emotional Reactions', as well as an interactive website – pathwaytohappiness.com which offers simple lessons and practices for understanding and then changing any belief systems or behavioural patterns that are not working for us.

These are just two suggestions that work for me but there are many other options available online – just google 'How to change my belief systems' and see which offerings resonate with you most – these will be the most effective for you.

Changing beliefs is challenging work but the results are profound. When we find the courage and time to change what isn't working for us, we are gifted with freedom which equals greater joy in our lives.

10

DON'T SHOOT THE MESSENGER

'Don't shoot the messenger' is the best piece of advice I have ever been given but it's also the hardest to practise as it means putting our ego on the shelf which it doesn't always like! Similar to the concept of the world being our mirror, if we can respect the messenger, then we are able to receive the valuable information they bring us.

So, who am I talking about when I ask you not to shoot the messenger? Our messengers are the situations or people in our lives who push our buttons – the people who hurt us, anger us, rip us off, shame us, irritate us and devastate us. They can be our husbands, our children, our neighbours, our friends, our colleagues or total strangers.

Paradoxically, these are also the people who can bring healing and freedom to our lives if we can look past their behaviour and focus solely on the feelings they stir within us.

When we can put our blame and anger aside and lean in to the emotions arising within us, we notice that all the distress, grief, anger and pain we experience can be distilled back to one of four basic human emotions. These are:

Rejection – the feeling of being spurned or discarded, of being irrelevant;

Abandonment – the feeling of being left by one we love and trust when we are in a vulnerable position;

Loneliness – the sense of being totally alone, without the support or love that is fundamental to the emotional health of all of us; and

Betrayal – of being hurt or let down by someone we trusted.

Any emotional discomfort can always be brought back to one of these four basic emotions – you just need to ask yourself which feeling is being triggered. Am I feeling rejected? Am I feeling betrayed? Am I feeling lonely? Am I feeling abandoned? It could be just one of these or it could be a combination of all four!

This practice is helpful because, as children, we have no real cognitive skills; we exist in a purely feeling state until we're about seven years old. So every negative experience we have is retained in the cellular memory of our bodies as an emotional wound.

Painful experiences in adulthood will always have a direct link back to a time we felt lonely, rejected, abandoned or betrayed as a child so whenever we're upset/angry/ bereaved, we need to sit quietly and ask ourselves when we have felt this way before, and over time we will often be led back to a painful memory from our childhood.

Sometimes these memories will arise immediately, sometimes they take hours, days or even weeks or months to enter our consciousness and that's fine, they will return if we set the intention to remember.

Once these painful memories surface, and we give ourselves permission to really feel the distress or anger for the hurt or enraged child we were, we are releasing these old wounds from our emotional body and giving ourselves the opportunity to heal. Healing can't take place until we acknowledge the distress we felt as a child.

Allowing ourselves the space to sit with painful memories isn't easy. Our natural inclination is to resist pain and leave distressing memories in the past. But if we're serious about living with joy, we have to examine and heal old emotional wounds. If we don't take the time to recognise and heal these wounds, there will always be someone to keep pushing that button until we resolve them.

I thought my biggest button was rejection. So often in my life I would be annoyed with someone who, in my perception, acted unfairly or poorly – it could be something as trivial as a motorist cutting across me or something major like a falling out with someone I love.

Once I stopped fixating on the situation and started asking myself which of the four key emotions it brought me back to, it was always rejection – the feeling that I didn't count, that I didn't matter.

So I started asking my Higher Self to show me when I had felt this way before. Within hours, memories started bubbling to the surface. Some of them were relatively insignificant but some of them were extremely painful, and I had to give myself the space to sit in my bedroom and cry for the distressed and frightened child I had been.

Acknowledging these painful memories validates them. It tells our inner child that we matter, that we are precious and that our adult selves will now look after our hurt inner child until he or she is fully recovered from any traumas that are inhibiting our capacity for joy.

A crisis is another way of being given an opportunity to heal core wounds in our emotional bodies. We've all heard the saying that if we don't pay attention to the whispers, then we'll hear a roar – that's what a crisis is. It is our soul's way of telling us that we have growth work to do, that we have old pain we need to release in order to heal and become whole again.

A crisis, no matter how big, will also always bring us back to one or more of these four basic emotions – loneliness, betrayal, abandonment or rejection.

I know this from experience. When my sister died, the panic I felt was indescribable. I couldn't function effectively and it was only once I started anti-depressant medication that I began to connect with the world again.

When I stopped the medication several years later, the panic resurfaced. My psychiatrist told me that behind anxiety, there is always anger. This was bad news for me as I wasn't confident in acknowledging and expressing anger, preferring to deny it even existed, but I knew if I wanted to manage the anxiety permanently, then I had to get in touch with the anger behind it.

I had no idea of the cause of the anger, or how to access it, so again I started talking to my Higher Self, asking that part of me that knows everything to show me when I had felt angry and anxious before. The process took several painful months.

The first memories to arise were of various times I had felt poorly treated but hadn't asserted myself. I had to put aside my blame and just be present with the anger and embarrassment I was feeling. It's not fun but if you can tolerate the distress and allow yourself to cry, the memories eventually lose their emotional charge.

The next lot of memories to arise came from my teenage years when I had been in some very unhealthy relationships. I had allowed myself to be abusively treated which reinforced the belief system that I wasn't valuable or truly lovable. Again, I had to move through the feelings of anger and shame, and just hold myself and allow myself to cry, sometimes for an hour or so on several occasions, before the memories lost their intensity.

When doing this practice, be gentle with yourself and remember that there is no right or wrong – our perception is the only one that matters and we need to allow ourselves to feel whatever arises. And don't allow guilt to get in the way.

One of the most painful aspects of my own healing was acknowledging my anger toward my sister Rachael for leaving me. The adult in me understood Rachael suffered with mental illness but when I stripped away the layers of shock and years of yearning for her, I was also furious with her. Unreasonable though it may be, the child in me felt totally abandoned. I was unbearably lonely without her and I didn't know how to fill the void and it took over twelve months for my anger towards her to subside.

When I asked my Higher Self when I had felt like this before, it took me back to my first years of school.

As a Prep and Year One student I experienced chronic separation anxiety and cried every morning. My teacher used to beat and shame me in front of the class. Her cruelty devastated me and as a young and terrified child, I was unable to verbalise my fear and rage so I simply internalised it, I didn't even tell my parents.

Rachael's death forced me to confront these feelings and the rage I had felt as a child and over time, I came to see that I had been an extremely sensitive and vulnerable child who had been terribly hurt. Once I recognised this, and created the opportunity to connect with and really grieve with the hurt child within me, I started to recover and the anxiety started to recede – or so I thought!

Grief and pain have so many layers – there will always be messengers to tell us when we have more personal growth work to do, and sometimes the messengers are the people we love most.

On the ten year anniversary of Rachael's suicide, I was set to have dinner with a very close friend however she cancelled at the last moment to attend a dinner party with some of her other friends.

I don't have the words to describe how abandoned I felt but I knew enough by then not to go in to blame, but to sit with the feelings that arose from the situation. The feelings of betrayal and abandonment were so intense but I just allowed myself to sit with them and literally cried on and off for 48 hours straight.

I asked my Higher Self when I'd felt like this before and was the feeling associated with rejection, loneliness, abandonment or betrayal? Again I was taken back to the first years of school and how abandoned I had felt by my mother and sister. While this wasn't the reality, it was how I felt at the time and so it is valid.

Having to leave the security and safety of my home for the classroom traumatised me and my sense of loneliness was acute. My girlfriend's abandonment of me at such a difficult time took me back to this place and once I recognised this, I could sit and hold the scared, small child within me until she started to feel safe again.

If we give our ego full rein, we go in to blame and lose sight of the healing opportunities we are being presented with. Had I gone in to blame with my girlfriend, it would have irrevocably damaged a valuable friendship and I wouldn't have realised how much trauma was still held in my body from those early years at school. Recalling that trauma, allowing myself to weep until I was spent, allowed the distress to permanently clear itself from my emotional body.

Being completely present with our anger/hurt/fear can be a distressing process because there is nowhere to hide. The whole point is not to resist which means experiencing the full force of the fury, sadness, fear or shame that we may have denied ourselves as children.

At times it can feel so overwhelming that we don't know what to do with ourselves but the difference between now and when we were young is that now we hopefully possess the cognitive awareness and self-soothing skills to comfort ourselves which we didn't possess as children.

Personally I find it helpful to scream, or to write down everything I am feeling (and then burn it), sometimes I put on boxing gloves and just beat the living daylights out of the punching bag. Allowing ourselves to really feel whatever comes up is a way of grounding the experience and then releasing it – permanently.

Anger is often behind anxiety and any distress we experience in our current lives can invariably be traced back to our childhood experiences. If we have the awareness and the courage to process the old pain, we can truly heal ourselves. It is an ongoing process that takes a lifetime, but layer by layer, we can release these soul wounds, which opens us up to greater joy in our lives.

This practice of not shooting the messenger, of not attaching blame to people or circumstances that trigger painful feelings, goes against our grain and our ego will always fight us on it.

Yet blaming others for our misery, no matter how great the injustice or disservice, is one of the biggest and most unhelpful habits we can fall in to. When we blame others, we are giving away our own power.

We always have a choice in how we react to any given situation. By accepting painful circumstances that arise in our life as an opportunity to feel into, and then clear old pain, we are taking responsibility for our own growth. We are opening the door towards healing and freedom. This is what mastery is all about and this is what leads to more joy in our lives.

The art of not shooting the messenger takes conscious effort and constant practice to refine. Even after ten years of practice, I can still go in to blame before I remember to just become the neutral observer – to allow the painful feelings to be present without attaching blame to the person who has brought them into my life to be released. But it's worth persisting as

I have found this practice to be the most helpful of tools for self-healing and joy.

I leave you with a poem by Jeff Foster, an amazing writer and spiritual teacher, which captures the essence of this chapter. You can find it at www.lifewithoutacentre.com.

DON'T BLINDLY FOLLOW YOUR FEELINGS by Jeff Foster

Feel your feelings. Don't push them away.

Yet don't rush to 'follow' them either.

Many feelings are simply old bodily memories from childhood.

Beautiful, precious, but not something to build your adult life upon.

Simply bow to feelings as they emerge.

Bless them with awareness.

In presence, let them move.

They are waves in your ocean.

They are your body's children.

They will come and go.

They are transient.

They are not the final truth.

When you allow feelings, they will not control you.

You are the container, never the contained.

You are the space for joy and sorry, bliss and boredom.

Don't blindly follow your feelings then.

Never be a follower.

Be a container. Be a space.

Sit with a feeling until you no longer feel compelled to act.

Let it move in you.

Until there is peace.

Then, from a place of slowness, quietude, presence, the rights words and actions, or non-actions, will flow naturally.

Follow the moment instead.

Follow the sacred breath.

Follow the field which never follows.

11

WE ARE FOUR BODY BEINGS

While we may be unaware of it, we are actually a four body being rather than just a single physical body. Our four bodies comprise of a spiritual, mental, emotional and physical body – all of which are inter-related and overlapping and impact greatly on each other.

The concept of a four body system is centuries old and simply illustrated in the Russian doll image below:

The *physical* body is represented by the smallest doll.

The *emotional* body sits within a hand span of our physical body and is represented by the doll second from the left.

The *mental* body is larger than both the physical and emotional bodies and is represented by the doll third from the left.

The *spiritual* body is represented by the largest doll. Our spiritual body envelopes all of our bodies, housing our entire being and our I AM presence.

We readily identify with our physical body because we can easily touch, feel and see it. Our physical body is affected by the quality of our food and lifestyle, as well as by what we think and feel. In the 1980's, Louise Hay revolutionised the way we consider this mind/body/spirit connection as her book, 'You Can Heal your Life', pioneered the concept into popular awareness and opened up a whole new world to millions of readers.

Taking this original concept one step further, our physical bodies are healthiest when we pay regular attention to our feelings rather than thoughts, and give ourselves time to process them. This can take practice because the busier our lives get, the easier it is to get caught up in the activity of our minds and thoughts rather than our hearts and feelings.

Our emotional body extends about one metre out from our physical bodies and houses all the feelings, positive and negative, we experience in our lifetime. The state of our emotional body determines our frame of mind.

If our emotional body is clear of trauma, anger and negative feelings, we will feel joyful and content; if our emotional body is polluted with hostility or pain, we will feel miserable.

When we are feeling unhappy, our natural inclination is to resist the discomfort. Typically we just want to feel happy again so we keep ourselves busy in order to avoid the unpleasant feelings. We drink, we smoke, we shop, we work too hard, we over-exercise, we occupy ourselves with all manner of distractions rather than sitting with uncomfortable or angry feelings.

In order to keep our emotional bodies healthy, it is helpful to acknowledge and allow feelings of distress, irritation or grief as they arise in any given moment, rather than resist them.

When we allow our negative feelings to be present, we gradually release the charge of the emotion and both our vibration and mood is lifted.

It is as simple and as difficult as allowing ourselves to experience the full impact of our feelings without blaming the person/situation which introduced the negative feeling. When we're busy blaming someone, we're not present with our feelings, we're busy judging. When we accept our feelings without blame, we are welcoming them, allowing them to be fully part of us. They sit still with us for a while and then they leave.

Spiritual teacher Jeff Foster suggests we view our negative or painful feelings as our children, as little beings which need to be recognised and held and comforted until they feel strong enough to head off again. He also suggests we view our feelings as little birds. Little birds that are present and making noise and we just observe them, listen to them, love them, and then they fly off. He suggests we love all our feelings, which I found to be great advice. If we love them, we honour them. When something is honoured, it finds its place. When something is denied, it is still present – it is just ignored until we deal with it.

The third largest doll represents our mental body, the home of our ego. Our mental bodies are governed by our minds and they can be rigid and restricting if we give our ego full rein.

Our mental bodies can be our best friend or worst enemy, depending how much power we give our ego, our human mind. We all have times when our mind runs away with us, when we judge and blame other people or situations for all manner of things.

To keep our mental bodies healthy and to optimise joy, we need to be vigilant with our thoughts as they can keep us

stuck in negativity. Our thoughts are not the truth of who we are, they are only our ego, so we need to catch ourselves if we're being negative, judgemental, irritated or angry.

Again, we then need to stop and reflect on what we're feeling rather than thinking, as our feelings tell us where our agitation is coming from. In allowing ourselves to feel into the emotion – rejection, abandonment, loneliness, betrayal – without judgement, the emotion can be released or resolved.

When dealing with a major issue, I find it helpful to remember that while I am feeling angry, I am not anger. While I am feeling sad, I am not sadness – I am not my mind, I am so much more than that. I reach for my soul essence, my Divine self that lives in my spiritual body (represented by the largest doll), which knows that my true self is love, patience, expansion and joy.

From the vantage point of my spiritual body, my Higher Self, I can look at myself objectively and recognise it is just my mind/ego which is experiencing disturbance, it is not me. To be able to observe ourselves objectively is freeing. It gives us permission to feel whatever arises without attachment, and so uncomfortable feelings can pass far more quickly.

To be able to access the clarity and expansion that is a healthy spiritual body, we need to meditate or consciously connect with it daily. This regular connection with our true selves brings balance to our lives, it offers us valuable guidance through insights and intuition and it brings us joy.

Awareness of ourselves as four body beings is the best way to maintain our health. If we don't deal with wounds or discord in our spiritual, mental or emotional bodies, it will eventually work its way through to our physical bodies and we become ill or notice physical pain. Pain is our body's way of telling us we're out of balance, that something is wrong and we need to pay attention.

I learned this the hard way. In 2013 I was hospitalised on several occasions with heart and stomach issues after a lifetime of keeping myself frantically busy so I didn't have to reflect on distressing memories I had buried so deeply that I didn't even realise they were there.

But being ill was the catalyst I needed to stop living in denial. I started the slow and painful excavation of these memories, gently bringing them up to the light of day, tenderly examining them and learning how to really feel. It was a lengthy and difficult process but once I started, I slowly began to heal physically.

It can take time for us to understand the emotional cause behind a physical ailment; it can be terribly distressing to sit with painful feelings and often we'll want to give up because it's so excruciating, but it's worth persisting.

In being present to what is happening within our bodies, especially our physical and emotional bodies, we come to a deeper understanding of ourselves. This knowledge brings a profound sense of joy with it, it brings us a deep appreciation of who we really are and, dare I say it, we become excited about our lives and what we are creating.

12

BE WILLING TO FORGIVE

Living with joy requires our hearts and minds to be open. It requires an attitude of trust in the inherent goodness of life, and the only way to maintain this open mind and heart attitude is a willingness to forgive those who hurt us.

Yet when someone does the wrong thing by us, we can feel so hurt or angry that it seems impossible forgive.

Over time, any long-held resentment can affect our health, it definitely lowers our energetic vibration and if we refuse it let it go, we can become contracted and bitter rather than expansive and genial.

Our egos tend to cling to perceived injustices or slights and it can be a real challenge for many of us to learn how to genuinely forgive – there is no short cut or easy way. However, it is worth persisting with mastering this life lesson as forgiveness is essential if we wish to live a joyful, healthy life.

As Stephanie Dowrick, author of 'Forgiveness and Other Acts of Love' so wisely says, "Forgiveness is the most demanding of all qualities; in our world, it is also the most essential....To begin the process of forgiveness, you need to let go of the wish that the other person would understand what they have done and suffer for it. They may never understand. They may never suffer 'enough'. That must cease to be your business."

As there are times when I have found it hard to truly forgive those whom have really hurt me, I have spent a great deal of time reflecting on this topic.

I believe forgiveness is much easier when we receive a genuine apology. An apology means we have been heard, that our feelings are valued and that we matter. Receiving an apology validates and often soothes us and so we are more likely to forgive.

If we have been hurt but there is no immediate apology, we often withdraw from a relationship or situation. Putting distance between us and our antagonist is our ego's way of protecting us, but resisting the temptation to walk away, and keeping dialogue open, honest and non-judgmental is the most effective way to resolve conflict.

This is really hard when both parties are experiencing intense feelings and reactions but if we can allow ourselves to be completely vulnerable and express how hurt we feel, we are more likely to create an opportunity for healing to occur.

If we have chosen our relationships wisely, our vulnerability and honesty will be appreciated, and we are able to move forward and the relationship grows.

If not, the relationship may break down permanently. This is where it gets tricky because even if we never see the other person again, I believe it is still wise to practise forgiveness, even when it feels impossible, for the simple reason that "revenge and hatred weaken you… to begin to forgive strengthens you" (Stephanie Dowrick).

When we don't forgive, the wound sits in our emotional body and the hostility and pain can move into the physical body and jeopardise our health over time.

So, how do we forgive someone who has no interest in repairing the relationship? How do we forgive when our differences seem irreconcilable? How do we forgive if the discord is with a close family member or friend where automatic behavioural patterns and responses are so engrained and it can be difficult to express ourselves as we would like, and so we just simmer quietly with resentment or hurt?

My only tried and true method is the Ho'oponopono – meaning 'to make right'. It is a Hawaiian healing technique which was practised by psychiatrist, Dr Hew Len, at the Hawaiian State Hospital where he indirectly healed a ward of prison inmates suffering from various degrees of mental illness.

Similar to the concept of the world being our mirror, Dr Hew Len's method works on the premise that all disturbance we experience or observe is a part of us and so we are responsible for the healing of it – even if the other party has no awareness of, or interest in healing.

Dr Hew Len cured these prisoners without meeting a single one of them. He simply studied their files, and based on his belief that their personal disturbance was somehow a reflection of his own, he set about the Ho'- oponopono practice.

He didn't have to understand the nature of their mental illnesses; he didn't have to know the origin of their condition. He simply trusted the philosophy that we are all aspects of God, of the one consciousness, of the one shared and Divine Intelligence, and so where there is disturbance in one element, there is disturbance in all. He believed that in recognizing the prisoners as a reflection of himself, and doing the healing work on himself, that he could heal the inmates. And he did. The ward closed down after Dr

Hew Len had applied the Ho'oponopono practice to all prisoners and they were eventually released.

The practice is as simple as saying the following four simple lines consistently and sincerely until the situation resolves itself and we find a sense of peace. It sounds impossible but it works! To quote Stephanie Dowrick again, "In thinking about forgiveness, understand that it offends the rational mind. It is a Divine quality that human beings can and must learn to practice." The four lines of the Ho'oponopono are:

> *I'm sorry*
> *Please forgive me*
> *I love you*
> *Thank you*

They translate as:

I'm sorry – I am acknowledging the pain I feel, I'm hurting, I'm sore.

Please forgive me – I recognise we are part of a shared agreement and I am taking responsibility for my part in this, conscious or unconscious.

I love you – my Higher/Divine Self understands we are both Source energy. By recognizing our mutual connection to Spirit, I acknowledge we are both worthy of Divine love and healing and trust this is occurring.

Thank you – I accept and allow the energy to shift between us and am grateful this is so.

The Ho'oponopono is a technique that demands trust as it seems implausible that these four simple lines could shift major trauma or angst but whenever I feel so furious, so hurt, so distressed and incapable of forgiving, this is my 'go to' solution.

Saying the four lines of the Ho'oponopono is a blind call for grace, for the intercession of the Divine. I know that whenever a situation feels beyond me, beyond my forgiveness or understanding, that this prayer brings me relief.

I use it to help clear major life trauma as well as on any other occasion when I am lacking understanding, patience or compassion.

I also use it when I am in need of self-forgiveness: when I remember times from my past when I have acted with cowardice or lack of integrity and I cringe with shame at the hurt I have inflicted on others.

Rather than allowing my ego to ruminate on negative thoughts or feelings, I commit to saying these four lines around the painful situation. It is a heart-felt intention to clear whatever pain or distress I am experiencing or witnessing, and somehow I am always gifted with an insight about action I need to take, or with a sense of peace or release around the discomfort.

It will feel strange at first but again, it's a case of fake it until you make it. When we keep saying those four lines with loving intention around any painful scenario, we will find resolution. Sometimes the anger or negative feelings will clear within hours or days. For a major life crisis, it can take months of saying the prayer but it works, especially in instances when there is no resolution or closure with the other party. The morphic field and intention of the prayer neutralises the negativity we feel and over time we find that the angst has settled. (Google www.hooponopono.org for more info.)

For readers who prefer a more philosophical approach, I love Eckhart Tolle's approach to forgiveness which is the willingness to see through the ego of our opponent to their inherent light, which is identical to our inner essence.

This is a similar philosophy as the Ho'oponopono but rather than an intentional mantra, it relies on us having the mental discipline to put our egos aside and consciously look for the divinity in others that reflects our own.

This concept is touched upon by Marianne Williamson in Oprah's Super Soul Sessions (http://www.supersoul.tv/%20supersoul-sessions/marianne-williamson-the-spiritual-purpose-of-relationships) when she discusses the fact that fundamentally, we are all the same. We are all aspects of Source energy and as such, we are all precious, all valuable – none of us is better than the other and we have no right to assume as much.

When we consciously and regularly practise this awareness of the divinity in all people, we become more adept at moving into the space of forgiveness. Even if forgiveness is elusive, at least we are doing our best to move beyond our egos which are always at the core of any disturbance.

When we go in to blame, when it is 'someone else's fault', we give all our power away. When we can trust that any discord we experience is either a reflection of ourselves or an opportunity to move beyond ourselves and look for the best in someone – then we are on our way to a happier life.

The bottom line is that forgiveness equals freedom and only we have the power to give that to ourselves.

13

LISTEN TO THE MASTERS

Exploring the great spiritual traditions through either the ancient texts or modern day interpretations, can bring great inspiration, great understanding and as a result, great joy.

While the texts of various traditions vary, the essence is generally the same – that we are all aspects of the same Source energy, of God.

Through the spiritual masters, we learn how to connect with our soul, our Divine Self, our God or Higher Self through meditation, spiritual practices or creativity. When we connect with this Source energy, we are merged with all that is light, with all that is pure, with all that is love. If we do this regularly enough, we are able to reach and maintain a higher vibrational state of peace and relaxation, with greater ease and for longer periods of time.

In connecting with this Source energy, we acknowledge the universal life force that surrounds us all, a conscious, living presence that is there beside us and within us every moment of every day, unconditionally loving us and if we will allow it, manifesting with us.

In connecting with this presence with gratitude daily, we come to feel precious in a way we never have before. We come to understand the magnificence of our being and our appreciation of ourselves increases.

We start to trust that we are never alone. We begin to delight in the smallest of interactions with people, animals and nature.

We start to become more present in our lives, and our spirit becomes lighter. If we connect with this Source energy regularly, we come to understand our life's purpose, our life's truth – and when we're living our truth, we're joyful.

When I was struggling through my thirties, I felt very isolated even though my husband was really trying to make me happy and there were plenty of family and friends to fill daily life. I had no real idea of who I was or what my life purpose was and this lack of personal identify meant I felt extremely unfulfilled and dissatisfied. I knew it was my soul crying out to be heard but I had no idea how to listen to it.

Listening to the masters encourages us to think big.

It connects us with our true nature, with the beauty of our human spirit and the joy that is our birthright.

After setting the intention to find inspiration and joy in my life and making the appointment to see Barbara, the first thing we did was an archetype chart reading (www.archetypechartreadings.com).

Barbara's archetype chart very clearly showed me what was working in my life, what wasn't and how to fix it. Where I needed assistance, her wisdom, healing practices, honesty, infinite gentleness and compassion encouraged me to keep searching for my own truth, to keep clearing old pain and belief systems that no longer worked for me and to start really knowing and loving myself.

This is what the spiritual masters do for us. They open the doors to our own knowing and the infinite power within us. They teach us that we are the creators of our own lives.

The works of contemporary masters such as Wayne Dyer, Eckhart Tolle, Mooji, Deepak Chopra, Brene Brown, Oprah Winfrey, Jeff Foster, Maureen Moss, Esther Hicks, Miguel Ruiz, Carolyn Myss and Marianne Williamson are great starting points if you are looking for inspiration.

The works and writings of these teachers are all readily available through a Google search and it's just a matter of looking at their website and seeing if their philosophy or interpretation resonates with you. If it does, keep reading!

Visit www.ted.com for inspirational viewing or www.supersoultv.com for 20 minute sessions with wonderful presenters, each of whom offers pearls of wisdom and inspiration.

The world offers us so much when we open ourselves to the hard earned knowledge and life lessons of others. Listening to the modern masters – those whose philosophies are aligned with the ancient spiritual texts and truths – connects us with Source/God and with ourselves.

When we listen, study and meditate on their words often enough, we begin to understand that: we are all unique aspects of the one whole; we are all pure consciousness; whilst we live in a three dimensional world which we can see, hear and touch and is full of duality –right and wrong, good and bad, happy or sad – our purpose is to actually embrace all feelings and experiences, rather than just the happy or positive ones, and always choose to re/act with love; our daily challenges are opportunities to move away from the judgement and blame of the third dimensional, physical world and lift our awareness to the fifth dimension of unity consciousness. In the fifth dimension we are aware of our individual I AM presence. The fifth dimension is where we maintain a conscious connection to our Spirit Self and an awareness of the God/Goddess within all beings.

When we transcend our minds to connect with our Spirit, we realise that we are not just our physical bodies, we are not just our thoughts or physical experiences – we are infinitely more than this.

We are spiritual beings having a human experience and when we get in touch with our soul essence, through meditation or spiritual practices, our daily struggles fall into perspective, we see they are just a tiny aspect of who we really are. When we begin to know our own spirit, we experience unspeakable joy and a sense of expansion.

Deepak Chopra defines this spiritual experience as: Transcendence Emergence of platonic (Plato) values Loss of fear of death. Chopra says that when we can practice stepping outside the mind and taking the position of witness, we access our 'presence' which is expansive and peaceful, generous and loving.

In this 'presence' state we find balance, we find freedom and we find joy. We understand that this 'presence', this God Self, is all that matters and we start marvelling at how powerful we really are and become the creators that our souls know us to be. (See http://www.oprah.com/own-supersoulsessions/deepak-chopra-belief-creates-reality-video for the full discussion).

If you have time, there is also a terrific YouTube account of one woman's near death experience and how it connected her with this concept of being one with all that is, and the peace and unspeakable that joy that comes with it. This interview can be viewed at https://www.youtube.com/watch?v=qX803D_cofI

No-one can give us this understanding. The ancients, the modern masters, they simply offer us this knowledge and the choice is up to us if we wish to receive it, to accept it and to practise it.

As Barbara often says, this inner work is not for the faint hearted. Mastery takes dedication and commitment. It's hard work and it's often two steps forward and one step backward but once we start to connect with this part of ourselves, it makes it all worthwhile.

14

CONCLUSION

There is a saying that we teach what we most need to learn – the irony of this truth wasn't lost on me as I wrote each chapter!

I started on this book because I wanted people to have access to the philosophy and skill set that changed my life, but in hindsight I can also see it was also a test of my commitment to these practices.

Whilst I was writing the last few chapters, I was delivered some devastating news. It rocked me to my core and shattered the foundation on which I have built my life. Ten years ago, it would have brought me undone but the discipline of drawing on the practices in this book, every day for the past ten years, has changed me. I am no longer scared of what I feel – I know rage and grief always pass and I have learned I am strong enough to tolerate them.

I am sure it was no accident I was given this painful news as I was writing this book. It was a daily reminder that I had to go within and allow myself to feel, rather than think. It was a reminder to find time daily to do something that I loved. It was a reminder to start reframing rather than blaming. It was definitely a time to listen to the Masters to gain a greater perspective. It was a time to evaluate and change many of my belief systems. Most of all, it was a reminder to practise forgiveness.

As I reviewed each chapter, I realised how much I rely on these techniques, how much I trust the underlying philosophy I have been taught. They have given me a framework for healing and sustained me during one of the toughest times of my life. They have given me a much greater understanding of myself and the anxiety that has plagued me since I was a child. Because of the techniques in this book, I am now strong enough to pick up the pieces and I know how to put myself back together again.

I have realised that whilst I adore my family and friends, I am no longer reliant on them for a sense of personal security – I feel confident in my own ability.

I am no longer dependent on the approval of others to make me feel worthwhile – I now see myself for the infinitely precious being I am.

I am no longer willing to please others at the cost of my own needs or integrity.

And as I write this last chapter, I finally know what my own truth is and feel brave enough to speak it out aloud. For me:

The human experience is all about duality and contrast and we call every experience in for our own growth;

It is not about being right, being happy or being comfortable all the time – it's about learning to allow and embrace every feeling;

Every distressing circumstance, no matter how harrowing, is an opportunity to release old pain and trauma;

Being totally present with painful memories or feelings, rather than resisting them, is the fastest way to release them;

It is only from a position of self-responsibility, not victimhood, that we can effect positive, lasting change;

True joy comes from a deep understanding, acceptance and appreciation of ourselves;

We have to honour our own feelings first and foremost;

When we are gentle and loving with ourselves, we can love others more deeply;

We are all connected, precious parts of the one whole;

A sense of purpose, based on generosity and love, gives valuable meaning to our lives;

Our heart is the best navigation tool we will ever have and it's vital we listen to its guidance.

Life is a full and varied experience with happiness and sorrow, love and resentment, hostility and peace spontaneously arising along the way.

Despite this duality, I believe we can cultivate a deep sense of joy within ourselves – a sense of joy that is still present even when our lives appear to be falling apart.

The practices in this book create the space for us to come to know our true natures, the beauty of our spirits and the joy that springs naturally when we access this part of ourselves.

When we start to experience our lives from this perspective, the vantage point of our soul, we begin to welcome and appreciate all that we are and all that the world has to offer – the good and the bad, the black and the white.

We start to find joy purely through existence. I trust this book will open doors for you and I leave you with a poem that captures the essence of this book:

THE GUEST HOUSE

by Jalaluddin Rumi (as translated by Coleman Barks)

This being human is a guest house.

Every morning a new arrival.

A joy, a depression, a meanness, some momentary awareness comes as an unexpected visitor.

Welcome and entertain them all!

Even if they're a crowd of sorrows, who violently sweep your house empty of its furniture, still, treat each guest honourably.

He may be clearing you out for some new delight.

The dark thought, the shame, the malice, meet them at the door laughing and invite them in.

Be grateful for whoever comes,

Because each has been sent as a guide from beyond.

ACKNOWLEDGMENTS

With deepest gratitude:
To Rach – for every precious minute of our life together;
To Samuel – for your infinite kindness, sensitivity and devotion which has brought me such happiness and healing;
To Simon – for your huge heart which understands mine, for your willingness to do whatever it takes with such good humour and grace and for your enduring love – thank you.

BIBLIOGRAPHY

Abraham-Hicks Publications, 1997, Abraham-Hicks, viewed 3rd March, 2011, http://www.abraham-hicks.com/lawofattractionsource/

Burton B, 2016, Sunshine and Snowfall, viewed 20th Sep- tember, 2015, https: //https://www.holstee.com/blogs/mindful-matter/73474117-sunshine-and-snowfall

Cameron, J, 1992, The Artist's Way, Jeremy P. Tar her/ Putnam, New York.

Dowrick, S, 1997, Forgiveness and Other Acts of Love, W. W Norton and Company, New York.

Foster, J. 2007, Life without a Centre, viewed 23rd February, 2016, http://www.lifewithoutacentre.com

Hay, L, 1984, You Can Heal Your Life, Hay House, Australia.

Hicks, E. & Hicks, J. 2006, The Law of Attraction, HayHouse, California.

How to practice the Law of attraction? Mike Dooley (Jan 5 2013) YouTube Video, added by Lilou Mace [online] Available at https://www.youtube.com/watch?v=8-7Zs-XALDM (Accessed 16th January, 2016)

Keys Jr, K, 1973, Handbook of Higher Consciousness, Love Line Books, Oregon.

Krystal, P, 1998, Cutting the Ties That Bind: Growing Up and Moving On, Weiser Books, Boston.

Modern Media, 1996, The Foundation of I, INC|Freedom of the Cosmos, viewed 22nd September, 2013, https://www.hooponopono.org/

Briggs, M. & Jung, C. 2010, Personality Page, 30th June 2015, http://www.personalitypage.com/

Oprah, 1998, Oprah, viewed 2nd January 2013, http://www.oprah.com

Oprah, 2015, Super Soul TV, viewed 13th November 2015, http://www.supersoul.tv

Osteen, P.J. 2015, OPRAH'S LIFECLASS: How Words Can Determine Your Destiny, viewed 10th of

November 2015, http://www.oprah.com/oprahs-lifeclass/pastor-joel-osteen-on-how-words-can-determine-your-destiny-video

Present! - Amy Call's Near-Death Experience (September 24, 2014)

YouTube Video, added by KMVT [Online]. Available at https://www.youtube.com/watch?v=qX803D_cofI& (accessed 20th of April 2016)

Secret Weapon, 1998, The Enneagram Institute, viewed 24th June 2016, https://www.enneagraminstitute.com/

Super Soul TV, 2015, Deepak Chopra: Belief Creates Reality, viewed 28th February http://www.oprah.com/own-supersoulsessions/deepak-chopra-belief-creates-reality-video

Super Soul TV, 2015, Marianne Williamson: The Spiritual Purpose of Relationships, viewed 28th February 2016, http://www.oprah.com/own-supersoulsessions/marianne-williamson-the-spiritual-purpose-of-relationships-video

www.ingramcontent.com/pod-product-compliance
Lightning Source LLC
Chambersburg PA
CBHW050318010526
44107CB00055B/2296